Flatlined 2 NGauge

DeWayne D. Rembert

To Steve,
Thanks for your support
Cuz! Love Ya man!

Dewayne R.

DeWayne D. Rembert

Copyright © 2018 DeWayne D. Rembert

Published By: www.PublishedAdvantageGroup.com

FLATLINE 2 ENGAUGE

Flatline 2 ENgauge simply means to die to sin (self) and become alive to God through Christ Jesus so that we may engage this culture without compromising the gospel. The scriptures for the concept comes from Romans 6:11 and Acts 17:16-34. My prayer is that God will use this book to raise awareness among His people, that they would be watchful and attentive when it comes to paying attention to those He's placed around them, especially children.

Even though I smiled a lot and pretended everything was okay ok, I was dying on the inside. For me to have my mom be in and out of the house, having no father in the home, my grandmother's memory fading, and me witnessing my uncles under the influence of alcohol more than I saw them sober, having all that going on, I was obviously not okay. ok. One of two Two things that were evident in my life. One, the church didn't know how to biblically engage me or my friends or, two, they didn't care. Either way, we needed to dialogue about it.

Now that I am an adult Christian, I try to be watchful of children that I have the opportunity to come in contact with. If I'm aware of a broken family structure, I try to at least ask how are they really doing? Do you need any help with anything? I don't want anything from you, I am a Christian and this is what we do. What are your interests in life?

The reason why "ENgauge" is spelled the way it is, is because if we are going to engage the culture without compromising the gospel; the bible has to be the gauge. The Word is the true gauge of reality.

CONTENTS

ACKNOWLEDGMENTS

First and foremost, I would like to thank my Lord and Savior, Jesus the Christ. In the process of putting this book together I realized how blessed I really am. Lord, you have spared me and set me aside for your work! I could never have done this without the faith I have in you! You are my everything!

To my lovely wife, Leslie: For the first time in 42 years, I am speechless! I can barely find the words to express all the wisdom, love and support you've given me. You are my #1 fan and for that I am eternally grateful. I married way up and out of my league.

To my children, Devin, Dorian, & Journi: What can I say? I am 100% convinced that I have the best children in the world. I have been blessed to be a dad for 16 years and I have never had to go to bed stressed about my children. You are respectful, loyal, and great role models. I love each of you dearly.

I also thank the Lord for my in laws, Fannie Thomas and George Thomas. My father in law Jimmy Smith. I thank God for Charles Mc Shane, Latechia McShane, Kenneth Mc Shane, Darius White, Rayvell Smith, Josephine Smith.

To all my friends and family. I thank God for my wonderful sisters Sharon, Meka, Paula, & Jaquisha. You all are the best sisters a brother could have. I am so thankful that you all were able to forgive me for mistreating you all when I didn't know Jesus. I didn't realize the gifts you were. I have been blessed with a lot of friends! So, I am not going to try to name names because I would take up pages. Nevertheless, I do want to recognize bodies. I thank God for the Anointed Warrior Hill Family, Hampton Inn Family, Strong Tower at Washington Park family, Flatline The Movement, Montgomery Baptist Association, Frazer United Methodist Church, Montgomery Public Schools, First Baptist Montgomery, Linden High School, Alternative Ministries, and all of the supporters of the ministry. We love you all and pray God continued blessings upon you all.

Dewayne Rembert

FOREWORD

As you read this gripping tale of one of God's chosen ambassadors ask yourself this question. What is the prerequisite for evangelistic outreach? What are the names of the courses you take? Where are these classes held? Where do you serve as an intern? What mission trip do you embark upon to learn what God intends for you to know for the work he has called you to.

I met Dewayne through a mutual friend who was awestruck with his outside the box ministry known around the city of Montgomery as Flatline. Years later I moved from Florida to Montgomery to serve as Head Football Coach at George Washington Carver High School which served the low socioeconomic west side. In the interview I talked to the committee about the importance of having a team chaplain, someone who was not your typical youth pastor. They smiled and told me about Dewayne. I was extremely excited to have the opportunity to join him as we took on the task of leading young men to Christ and disciplining them.

As I got to know Dewayne as a person I realized I had never met anyone quite like him. I knew people who did not grow up going to church on a regular basis but started a relationship with Christ as an adult, but he was different. I knew radical guys who performed hip hop music with a biblical message, but he was unconventional. I knew African American guys who could speak to the inner city and the country club, but this was different from anything I had seen.

Dewayne is a swiss army knife for Christ. Not only equipped with a gift of communicating the gospel message to different cultures, but he possesses a unique blend of humility and confidence. His life experiences have shaped his ministry into a microcosm of what heaven looks like. These experiences have caused him to challenge us to die to our self; to flat line in order to engage the culture.

This concept is unconventional, uncomfortable and unfortunately uncharacteristic of most believers. The concept found in *Flat Lined to Engauge* is essentially what Paul was saying in his letters to the early church. Those thirteen letters challenged, inspired, condemned and equipped the early church to engage the culture.

Like Paul Dewayne has had a radical encounter with Christ that will impact the kingdom forever. I am so glad he wrote it down for us to read.

Willie Spears
Author, Coach, Preacher, Speaker
Williespears.com

CHAPTER 1
GRANDPA'S CHEST

It was the summer of 1978 or 1979, and I was three or four years old. I remember Lying on the chest of a tall man, I was experiencing what felt like the best moment of my life. Nevertheless, it just faded away. I don't remember seeing him again. I don't know why, but I didn't ask where he went.

My next memory was of an old lady who was strong in my eyes. Everyone called her "Daughter." She was awesome! She called me "Shine!" She allowed me to sleep on her chest! I remember her as my grandmother and she introduced me to my mother, Rose. I really didn't know how to explain how I felt about Rose at that age. All I know was that my grandmother told me that I always had to respect her no matter what. It didn't matter what my grandmother told me to do, I knew I needed to do it.

I was still four or five years old, not yet starting school, and playing outside while Rose chopped wood for the fire to keep us warm. An ax handle swept toward my face, the ax flew off the handle. Then, there's this excruciating pain in my face, and blood runs down it. The next thing I see is

Rose getting a whipping.

That was weird to me even though I couldn't explain it. That was my first real memory of Rose. I knew she was my mother, but I didn't see her that much. All of our water supply was from a well in the backyard, and I used to go outside with Rose to get water to drink and wash up. I also remembered the bathroom being outside. We had a garden with corn and okra. There was also a hen house where I would go in sometimes and watch the chickens hatch their chicks.

There were times when my grandmother and I would walk all the way to town, which took a very long time. I'd look up at her as she held my hand. *Wow, she's everything,* I thought. Strong. Smart. She loved me. I knew she was special to others as well because other guys came into the picture. I remember the school bus dropping three guys off at our house and only two lived with us. She would make them go to this table in the corner and do their homework. Then, they were able to go outside. The other guy's house was over the hill.

Now, I'm five and it was time to go to school. I remember it so clearly, on the first day of kindergarten, I dressed up in a suit. I remember Grandma taking me to school and I remember seeing her leave. It was scary, but exciting.

School was going along fine until my teacher had another adult sit in the class, and she began to do things to me that I did not understand. She grabbed my hand and put it in her pants. I was so scared and I just didn't think this was right, but I didn't tell anyone.

After that, I remember my first lie. I thought that I was going to break wind (fart), but I must have had diarrhea because I messed on myself and told my teacher that I hurt my finger. She gave me a wet paper towel and I wrapped my finger and stayed in the office for the remainder of the day. When I got home I told my grandmother what really happened and she cleaned me up and told me not to do that again. She said I knew better and to go to the bathroom and that if this happens again I will get a whipping.

CHAPTER 2
THE CHURCH HOUSE

On Sunday mornings, we attended church. We would get all dressed up, and then someone would pick us up. Once we arrived, I knew I would get a peppermint and get to lay my head on her lap. The thing that stuck out to me was there were only two or three men there. So, unbeknownst to me, I thought church was for old ladies. I can't remember where the men interacted with me. When I first began to go, I didn't remember any children my age. Did church even cross my mind after I left? Not that I could remember. It was something that my grandmother did and wanted me to do.

Something always happened, though. I had to speak to this one particular lady no matter what. According to my grandmother, she'd learned this was my other grandmother. This lady told me later on in my life that her son was my father. She was a very nice lady, but at that time I used to wonder why I had to speak to her even if I didn't personally speak to the other ladies. Nevertheless, I knew not to question my grandmother.

CHAPTER 3
WARPED MANHOOD

At the same time, seeing other men come around that I learned were my uncles. My first memory of them was seeing them staggering while trying to walk. Then, I remember hearing Rose say "sit your drunk a** down somewhere." I learned that this was what drinking alcohol did to people. I later learned that it was called being drunk. I used to wonder how drinking benefitted people. The times when they weren't staggering, they were complaining about a headache from drinking too much. In my mind, I used to think there's got to be something I am missing. This is confusing.

A few times, one of my sober uncles would give me money out of a Clorox bottle he kept under the seat of his truck. I still looked up to him because I knew he worked. At that time, my uncles were the men that were around me the most. One of them lived down the street, but he used to come by the house every day to pick up his mail. I heard him talk about his children, but I never saw them. Then I would think to myself, I wonder if his children feel the way I do, feeling bothered without a dad. Each time I would overhear him talk about his children living in another city, and I never saw them. It gave me a weird feeling toward him. Nevertheless, I wasn't going to say anything because that was grown folks' business. There were times when I heard people asked Rose who my dad was and she would say, "I'm his momma and his daddy." This confused me. One time she asked me to confirm what she said by saying, "Ain't that right, Wayne?"

"Yes, ma'am." I walked away with a tight burning in my chest.

CHAPTER 4
DADDY PAIN

Nevertheless, with all this confusion going on, I am still doing well in school.

Now, I am in the fifth grade and the longing for a father grows to the point of anger. Nevertheless, I'm still not talking about it. It's really clear now that some of my friends have dads in their homes and I don't. Some of the children even joke about me not knowing my dad. I lie and say I do know my dad, my words preceded by profanity.

I wasn't innocent with throwing jokes on others, most of the time. I'm starting them now. This is how I felt better about my situation. I need to put somebody else down. The fact remained that when they threw the daddy jokes, they actually hurt. I mastered hiding it, though. The most hurtful thing about the daddy jokes was not only did I not have one living in my home, but I really had no clue who he was. So, I finally asked Rose, "Who is my daddy?"

"I am your father," Rose said.

"You can't be my daddy," I said. "Please, just tell me who he is."

Rose sighed. "All right. His name's Michael and he lives in Birmingham. I haven't seen him since I got pregnant with you."

Oh, I didn't believe her, but I never told her. I was determined to make myself accept the fact that he didn't want me. And I didn't care.

Now, I have two sisters, and they have a father that stops by and sees them on occasion and brings them gifts. He was nice to me, but I knew he wasn't my father. It showed clearly during the summer when he would buy their school clothes and not buy me any. Of course, Grandma got me clothes. He would feed me if we went out together. He was the first person to take me to the movies.

Sunday rolls around again and we are in the church house. Here I am secretly hoping that someone would pull me aside and ask me how I was really doing instead of assuming I was okay. I even walked over and stood next to some men gathered outside, conversing after church, hoping someone would try to have a serious conversation with me. After a while, I said forget it. There were times where I stopped assuming that they were assuming I was okay and came to the conclusion that they didn't care. Out of the three or four men that I saw at church, one of them I knew because he hung around with my cousin. My cousin called himself a player and I thought this guy was, too.

Other than greeting me, he never talked to me at church.

CHAPTER 5
REALITY CHECK

After visiting some other homes in the area, I realized we did a lot of things differently. Some of us were in the same boat, but some were different. In order for us to have water to bathe, drink, and cook, we had to draw it from the well in the backyard or we put buckets on the side of the house to catch it from the roof.

Also, our house didn't have a bathroom. We had to go to use our outhouse. Yes, this was '84 and '85. I saw so many flies and piles of other people's mess in the outhouse that most of the time I just held it. I also noticed as I went over to some of my friend's houses that they had a room with a bed. I knew that I didn't have a room. Since we did not have central heat, all of us slept in the room where the fireplace was so that we could stay warm during the winter. In the summer, we slept on the couch in the living room with the door open in order to stay cool because all the windows were nailed shut.

All the while I'm thinking: *I wish I could do more about our situation. Why aren't we getting help?*

Fear, lack of knowledge, and rejection crippled me. I

never mentioned how I really felt. Why are all my uncles drunk all the time? Where is my daddy? Does anyone care?

CHAPTER 6
GLIMPSE OF HOPE

So, flash forward to junior high school, the most confusing time of my young life. I wanted to be grown, but I still wanted to be Grandma's baby.

Then, I see this comedy show on television called *Who's the Boss*. I don't know, but for a moment, I believed that I wanted to be like the character Angela when I grew up. She was an advertising agent. She actually made a living by talking and coming up with ideas for commercials and companies. I was so blown away. She made enough money to hire a housekeeper, a former pro baseball player named Tony. It was a weird mix-up, too, because Tony's daughter moved into the house because his wife had died and Angela was divorced and had a son.

Tony and Angela had a thing for each other. Nevertheless, each time I watched the show I was more interested in her job than I was in the stories on the show. From the first time I saw this show, I knew I wanted to one day do something like that. I actually believed it for a minute. I said to myself that I am going to make a living with my mouth. My grandmother saw that I was into that show and why. She used to tell me "Wayne, you can be whatever you put your mind to." Her words helped me on many occasions when I wanted to just go and hide from life.

CHAPTER 7
UNLEASH THE BEAST

Even though I had Angela as my positive role model, it wasn't strong enough to keep me uplifted. I was witnessing things that disturbed me. First, I saw where my grandmother paid some men twenty dollars to take us to the laundromat in Myrtlewood, about six or seven miles from our house. Sometimes, she would hire some of them to take us to town to get food in Linden, about six to seven miles from the house, and give some of them twenty dollars also. I knew how much gas was and that was way too much. I would get so upset on the inside, yet I didn't say anything. All the while I'm piling all of this anger up inside of me at only eleven years old. I thought life for most men just wasn't good. It was like I was full of this secret anger, but crippled by fear to do anything about it. Granted, all of them didn't practice this.

Now, it's 1987 and I'm twelve years old and I get introduced to Ice T, a gangster rapper. On this white cassette tape was this song called "6 N the Mornin'."

Who is he? I thought. I heard this brave, tough, rich guy. That was the first time I heard the term "beeper." He was talking about beating somebody down which is really what I wanted to do because I saw my grandma get taken advantage of by swindling guys, in my opinion. My mother taken advantage of, my mother not telling me the truth about my daddy, our living situation, and my daddy letting me suffer like this, and now my grandma is starting to forget stuff.

Then, there was another scary moment that happened in junior high that injected fear in me. There was this professional that came to the school and ran tests on us. He concluded that I had scoliosis. He told me that by the time I'm forty I will be walking in a bent over position unless I received treatment. I remember going home and telling Rose, and she said "that da** doctor don't know what he talking about, ain't nothing wrong with you."

Well, I was scared and who was going to just up and take me to get checked out? What does that mean? Where would we go? So, I'm just going to try and forget it. Well of course, that doesn't work, and I think it crossed my mind every day.

Well, the good news was that I tried out for the basketball team, and made **it.** That was hard sometimes, because I always had to depend on someone else taking me home.

On top of that, I observed my grandmother's mind fading more and more, but we still go to church. While at church, as soon as we had a chance, my cousin and I would go to the car and listen to hip hop. No one ever checked to see what we were doing or what we were listening too. We heard the church songs, but they bored us. I couldn't remember one if you had asked me to sing a verse on Tuesday. It felt like two totally different worlds.

In my little mind, they didn't care to know about my world and I didn't care to know about theirs. Nevertheless, the things my grandma taught me from birth still remained in me. She said to always respect older people. So, disrespecting older people was out of the question no matter how I felt on the inside. There were people besides my uncles who were drunk all the time, but I was trained to still give them the highest respect. There were people who went to church, sang in the church while messing with women, yet I was stilled trained to give them the highest respect.

CHAPTER 8
REBELLION CREEPIN' IN

Fast forward to high school and my grandmother's mental health really began fading. I'm into hip hop now, and I'm acting out a lot of the lyrics as far as getting girls and even being tough. It's working. Now my walk is changing, my pants are lower, I'm speaking my mind. I'm mean to my sisters, all three of them. I'm getting a little popularity with the girls.

I started band in the ninth grade and liked playing the drums and the trombone with some of the pretty girls in band. So, I joined the band because Grandma was adamantly against football.

Now, I was pretty good at football when we would play after school or on weekends, but I was skinny. So, I became popular, but I didn't have the nicest clothes. Grandma did what she could. So, now I had an excuse to stay over after school because I had band practice. After band practice, we would go to the projects. I got to meet some guys that were out of school and they were fresh. They had on the British Knights (tennis shoes), the Levi's (jeans), the Starter caps (hats), and the fly shirts. I wanted some and found out that some of them would just go in the store and take them. "Man, it's really easy," they told me. "Just go in and snatch the pants off the hanger, roll them up, and stick them in your coat."

"That's it?" I said.

One of them nodded. "We'll distract the worker and just walk out."

Well, the first time I tried it, I got away with it. Then, I just couldn't stop. I would go in and take hats, shirts, and pants at the same time. It had gotten so bad, that I would burst into this uncontrollable laugh before leaving the store. Pretty soon, me and another guy in Linden who was also in the band were known on the block as two of the best thieves in Linden. Before you know it, I was stealing out of all convenience stores whether it was candy, chips, gum, wine or whatever. I didn't care if I had the money, I wasn't paying for it.

Then, I get into gambling. I learned how to play the card game called Tonk. Very quickly, I become addicted. My first time playing was for money and I won over thirty dollars. Nevertheless, I lost more than I won.

I had this little popularity thing going on, but I am still insecure about my size, my home situation, and I still want a dad. I tried out for the high school basketball team and made it.

A childhood friend also made the team and we spent a lot of time together. I used to love going over to his house after practice. It was the best. His mom was nice and his dad was super nice as well. His dad couldn't walk, but my friend simply adored him and whatever came out of his dad's mouth to him, it was solid. We used to eat dinner together at the table and then go in his room and play each other in basketball. He had this plastic goal over his room door. I was like, "Wow!" He has a room, a bed, color television and cable! Even though that was inspirational, I became jealous.

On top of all that, we were in a class where the class had to go into a pasture and study child birth and nutrition. There was this girl that was in the band with us that I secretly liked, but hadn't said anything to her. The teacher was using an example of getting pregnant by a healthy male. He actually used me as an example of the unhealthy male and compared me to a pretty well-built guy. He asked the girl who I secretly liked which one would be better to get pregnant by, him or me? She said him, obviously. Then, he said the likelihood of someone like me having healthy children would be slim to none. Right now, I am boiling on the inside! I let it go, but that was almost a breaking point for me.

Moving right along in high school, I enjoyed reading and English. Every other subject gets on my nerves. I could still remember Angela from *Who's the* Boss, but that dream was beginning to fade because I'm in high school and have no idea on how this is going to happen. I'm failing a lot of classes because I'm not trying, because deep down I'm thinking I'm too dumb and even if I had the chance to get out of here, I couldn't afford college.

CHAPTER 9
DON'T CARE ANYMORE

Looking back on the eleventh grade, I did not begin to take school or life seriously. I did my best to do my dirt while not messing up my grandmother's reputation. But then, the unimaginable happened. I and two other guys are in the hallway. One of the respected school administrators walked up to us. He began to talk to the guy on the right about getting his stuff ready for college, skipped over me, and began talking to the other guy about getting his paperwork ready for the military. He didn't even acknowledge me! At that moment, it was like he stuck a dagger in my heart and twisted it. Now, you would think this would motivate me to say in my mind "I'm going to show him," instead I heard a voice in my head saying "forget everybody!"

I knew guys around me who were dabbling in the drug game, but before that moment, I really said I'm not going that far. After his confirmation of my doomed life, I was like, why not, I'm not going to be anything anyway.

My gambling increased. Sometimes I would win and sometimes I would lose. Nevertheless, it took up most of my days. There were times I would lose hundreds of dollars from various activities that I came across the money with.

Now, I didn't understand how church was supposed to help me or if it was supposed to or not, but I did think that preachers were supposed to be highly respected. Well, one day a well-known preacher came into the gambling/shot house to sit down to gamble and drink. I knew something was wrong with what he was doing. Since my most vivid memory of church people outside of the church building was when a church lady told me to "get those earrings out of your ear boy, and pull up your pants. You're going to hell!" This drained any type of hope of possible good. I said to myself that if the preachers are bad, everybody else is probably bad.

I had this "down" homie who I was super tight with. In our hood, to this day, he is undefeated in street fighting. He was a loyal friend that would fight at the drop of a dime. Coupled with this; secret anger toward my father, my experience with this administrator at the school, this teacher telling me I will never have healthy kids, our living situation, and this preacher that has confused the mess out of me, I really didn't care about what happened to me.

Grandma's mind was gone anyway. There were many

fights that I normally got a few stomps in. On one particular night, at three in the morning, I accompanied a guy who'd been in a fight a couple of nights earlier. We were walking the streets after just leaving some girls. I looked back and saw the guys we had been fighting plus some more with a bat, chains, and who knows what else. We ended up knocking on this house owned by someone who knew us and told him what was going on. He let us in and then walked us to his truck with his shotgun and then took us to his aunt's house. I really believe if I had not looked back when I did, that they were going to hurt us really bad or even kill us that night.

That still wasn't enough to slow me down because I still lacked leadership and harbored all of this anger and hurt.

Another homie that came to me and said he knew of this "lick" we could make. Lick means easy, illegal money. He said that he knew of this camp house that was vacant that we could rob. It had a lot of guns in them and we could sell them. I remember being out that night on the block, really unsure where I was going to sleep that night, so I said "I'm down!" We get there, he's on one side of the camp house and I'm on the other, but I hear noise on the other side where no one was supposed to be. Immediately, I slid between the wall and the refrigerator and this fat white guy with a white tank top on holding a shot gun walked right past me. After he goes further into the other room, I take off running out of the camp house outside until I see this big tree to hide behind and say this to myself in a frustrated voice, "Why am I here?" I really felt like a slave that was being controlled by something. The guy I came with had left me! Therefore, I ran all the way back to the projects.

My life is going nowhere fast at this moment. So now, I'm asked to hold dope for dudes who're sliding me a few dollars every now and then, and I'm riding and driving around with a known neighborhood drug dealer. He had a nice car with rims and a rag on the roof with boom in the trunk. His car was a little fast car and we would street race at night. He would get us alcohol, take us to the club, and hook us up with women/girls. I knew any day could be that day when we would either get caught or robbed. A part of me just wanted it to happen because I was tired and so miserable on the inside. I was tired of faking. If I didn't fake it, in my mind, I wouldn't survive.

Then, I do get this other guy that lived out of town to come in and make attempts at that time to keep some of us out of trouble and off the corner. He would say, "if you're not on the corner when I roll up, I'll let you drive my car and I will fill it up with gas." That was huge for us because it was a sports car with rims with a nice system. In our town, hitting blocks was a big thing because most of the girls would be out walking in groups. Also, this guy was known for a more positive impact. So, he did begin to talk to a few of us about getting out and making something of ourselves.

Even though he talked to us about education, he still encouraged the player lifestyle. As a result of that, when I brought up how I was feeling, I sensed that I was coming across as weak, so I buried it again. I needed more, I just didn't know what that more was. Eventually, I made up in my mind that nobody has this "more" that I'm looking for except on television shows, so I was convinced it was not real.

CHAPTER 10
HIGH SCHOOL GRADUATION

In spite of all the skipping and lack of effort in doing my work, I graduated high school. I had gotten a little information on things I wanted to do but had little hope because we had no money. I didn't know about scholarships. No one told me or offered to help me when it came to the ACT or the ASVAB.

The first seven months after graduation, I returned to my grandmother's house and hid out so people would think I went somewhere. Eventually, I just could not take it anymore. I got bored because my regular day was getting up early in the morning with my uncle sitting on the backside of the house because that's where the sun shined. So eventually, I came out of hiding. I started hanging with the guys who were selling drugs, and I start selling. I didn't make much money, and I used to wonder if it was even worth it.

There was another moment in my life where I knew that should have been it. This guy and I went to Uniontown, Alabama to pick up an eight ball (3.5 grams of cocaine). On the way back on a two lane highway at 3 am, he spots a set of headlights about a mile ahead and says "oh sh**, it's 5.0." He then tosses the dope out the window.

Now, I'm looking at him like how in the world can he tell that that's the police that far ahead by just looking at headlights. Sure enough, the car meets us and turns on the blue lights and pull us over. The officer walks up to the car and says that this vehicle matches the description of a vehicle that was involved in a robbery earlier tonight. Then, the guy I was with seemed to have given him some type of signal and the officer let us go. He didn't asked to see ID, insurance, or anything. That whole situation was suspicious to me.

Nevertheless, the police made a bust a few weeks later, and my grandmother came to her right mind for about ten minutes. She said I needed to get out of there.

The guy who was at least trying to show us another way, came and got me and I moved to Montgomery. I left my grandmother's house with an IGA plastic bag with a pair of underwear and a t-shirt and the clothes on my back.

CHAPTER 11
THE MOVE

Then, in Montgomery, I found a job at Wendy's. I enrolled in Troy University. Things are seemingly looking up. I had made up in my mind that I must succeed because there is absolutely nothing for me to go back to in my hometown.

I came up with this plan that whatever no one is willing to do on the job, I will. I was so thankful to be able to buy food. For the first time, I had my own room where I can take a shower. I wasn't happy, but I was better off than I was. I still struggled with the secret pain of neglect and unworthiness. I still wanted to be affirmed as a person and a man.

One of the managers at Wendy's picked up on the fact that I was starving for leadership. He introduced me to Islam. He would take me in the freezer and teach me some of Islamic teachings from the Quran. It was very tempting because he was much nicer than the church people I had come in contact with. He took the time to sit down with me to teach me one-on-one. Nevertheless, I had questions that he couldn't answer. I had heard of heaven and I asked him how I could get there. He explained to me that it was paradise, and he was telling me how I had to live a righteous life. I felt the pressure of not really knowing what that meant. I would see him look and flirt with women the same way I did. In my mind, I thought he was not really living righteous. Nevertheless, I was starting to belong to something.

At this time, one of the other managers at Wendy's was Caucasian and very nice to me, so it was hard for me to swallow the whole white man is the devil concept. Now, I never really accepted any of the invites out to the mosque, but his spiritual beliefs were the most I had at that moment. I didn't quite know what the church people believed, but he made it known many times that they were wrong. Honestly, I didn't believe him completely, and I didn't know what church people really believed. Nevertheless, as soon as the white guy on my job disciplined and disrespected me, the idea of the white man being the devil became more real to me.

Then, the white guy who was friendly left Wendy's and got a job at a restaurant/bar that was connected to a hotel named Ramada Inn. He later reached out to me and offered me a part-time cleaning job. I accepted and as I got there, I met another brother who shared my views instilled from the guy at Wendy's.

CHAPTER 12
A REVOLUTION

At twenty, I was waiting on a revolution! I was ready to hurt some folks for oppressing us. I was looking for a fight. I was now ready to reveal and release this anger!

Despite all this, I was still doing well on the job. I moved from cleaning the floors to working the breakfast bar. This lasted a couple of years and then my boss promoted me to the banquet department.

Even though I earned decent money working banquets, I wanted more. One day, I went home to hang out and asked my grandmother for some money before I returned to Montgomery. She told me that my uncle was over her money. I went to ask him for some money, and he didn't want to give me any. I was so shocked because in my mind, I am in Montgomery trying to make something out of myself. I remember him saying to me that I needed to come back down here to work at the mill like my cousin.

I was so full of pride and anger that I slapped him in front of his wife and she told me to leave. At that time, I brought my girlfriend with me. She witnessed it, and I thought she was going to help me justify what I just did, but she told me I was wrong. I believed her, but I didn't know how to apologize. It was years later when I actually did apologize.

My mindset was that I was still a hustler. During this time, I got hooked up with this guy that I met at the bar, and he showed me how to make money selling bootleg CD's and knock-off clothing. Every Tuesday, a new CD would come out. We would go buy the original CD from the store on Tuesdays and duplicate hundreds of them at night. We would sell them for five dollars each, or five for twenty dollars. It was just like the drug game, but safer in my mind and somehow not so bad. We would give you one CD from a rapper that was in a large clique because we knew people would come back for more. R&B was selling a lot, too! Business was booming so well that when I rolled through certain neighborhoods, they would flag down the car begging for that new music. I even sold Gospel music and never listened to it. I knew about Kirk Franklin, though. We sold blues CD's. The biggest blues sales went to people who bought Gospel music and had some church affiliation. That was weird to me, but I didn't care, I just wanted the money. There were some days where we made five hundred to seven hundred dollars from music sales alone. Then, from the knock- off clothing, I could make another three to five hundred dollars through another contact in Montgomery.

CHAPTER 13
MYSTERIOUS HELP

Girls were easy, a little too easy. They were so easy that l
I actually used to tell the homies that I was going to get
some help. In my mind, the girls in Montgomery, Auburn,
and Tuskegee were so easy that I wanted a challenge. I
once was told when I first came to Montgomery that if I
had the chance to pull some girls in L.A or Miami, then I'd
be really doing something. I was told that would really be
living it up. This would be my climax!

So, I got the chance to go to Miami, Florida. My friends
and I arrived and we linked up with my roommate's high
school homies. He had a new Range Rover. We were
hitting the town, the strip, and the strip clubs. They even
mistakenly took us for celebrity rappers and one of the
homies for a player with the Miami Hurricanes. Well, you
can imagine how that night went. Nevertheless, after all
that, we got back to the room and I remember saying to
one of the homies, "Man, there's got to be more to life
than this!" I felt like if this was the peak, I don't want to
live anymore! It was empty!

For a while, I was pretending like I was having a good

time, but on the inside just wish I was alone somewhere in a room. I was miserable! Due to my selfishness, I had run off the girl I knew I could have had a future with. After this moment of borderline depression, I mustered up enough courage to call her. I thought maybe she was my answer to happiness. So, I called and she answered. We talked a good while. I asked her if we could we get together when I get back from Miami and she said yes! Hope rose in my heart.

CHAPTER 14
WHATCHA LOOKING AT?

Leslie and I get back together. She soon realizes this unresolved anger and insecurity. There were times she would be afraid to go anywhere with me because of the way I would stare at people or if you stared at me, I wanted to know what you were looking at. There were times that if we were at a traffic light and I catch a dude looking over into the car and he pulled off, I would chase him down to stare at him with a "What's up, homie?!" attitude. Nothing major ever jumped off from that.

I had this anger and this good girl along with about four more girls I was stringing along. I'm not promising them anything as far as a committed relationship, but I knew they would have been cool with it if I pushed it. Now, deep down I knew I wanted to only be with this one particular girl, but I was taught that you have keep one or some on the side. This is the only way I do not get hurt.

All this frustration is happening because I am always lying, hustling, and sneaking around. I was so unaware of how bad I was really living. I remember asking my girlfriend Leslie how she was paying her bills. I asked her because she had an apartment, but didn't have a job at the time. She responded with "you pay my bills. I save when you give me money."

CHAPTER 15
THE EXPLOSION

Although I had all this going on, I still managed to do a good job at the hotel. I no longer worked at Wendy's. I remember vividly working in the banquet department one day and we were having the biggest function in the city. With all this bottled-up anger, coupled with this information that I have been fed was untamable. It was only a matter of time before I exploded.

The day prior, I was playing basketball and sprained my wrist. I had to go to the doctor, and I had an excuse to be off work, but as I brought the excuse in to work, I was still going to try and help out. Nevertheless, while I was in our storage room gathering items to help assist with the banquet, unaware of my closeness, I heard my white boss (who's always been nice to me) say to another white lady "of all the days to get hurt, he gets hurt now."

I was more furious than I've ever been before! I stormed out of the storage room and went up to him and pointed my finger in his face while touching his nose and dared him to say another word! I was so out of it that I didn't care that there were many witnesses around. He would not say a word. I heard voices in my head giving me instructions that if he said a word to knee him between the legs and when he bends down, upper cut him. Even though I had been working there for about four years now, I quit because of that comment.

CHAPTER 16
THE FRONT OFFICE

I told Leslie what happened, thinking she was going to be on my side, but she explained to me how wrong I was. I knew she was right after I had calmed down, but I was too manly and had too much pride to go and apologize. I'd rather not have a jo than to apologize. About four days later, she convinced me to go back. Filled with pride, I still didn't apologize. I walked in and wrote my name on a timecard and just started working. The word got out to the manager about what I had done and to my surprise he came to me and apologized and asked if everything was good for me to return. I said yes and got back to work.

I was working banquets, but was also responsible for calming down brides if anything went wrong with the wedding reception, family members if something went wrong with family reunions, or the corporate leaders if anything went wrong with their corporate meetings.

Finally, after many praises from customers, I was feeling better about things.

The general manager wanted to speak to me about what's been going on and offered me a sales coordinator job in the front office and explained that if I did a good job as a sales coordinator, I could become a sales manager in two years. I had to be familiar with Microsoft Excel and Microsoft Word. Well, as flattering as that was, I didn't think I could do that. Fear gripped me! I didn't take computer in high school and the college courses I had taken so far didn't require me to use a computer. I shared this opportunity with Leslie, but I was certain I was going to turn it down. Surprisingly, she said something to me that I had never heard before from anyone! She said "Wayne, you are smart!" When she said that it was like fire ran through my body! So, I changed my mind. I didn't have any dress clothes for an office job. Thrilled for my opportunity, she bought me some slacks, shirt, and a tie.

CHAPTER 17
CHURCH AT WORK

I was then the sales coordinator for the hotel. My job was to answer the phones, gather information, and pass this information on to the director of sales. She would then make contact with the potential client and book the event. Then, she would give the information back to me and I would create contracts and file the events in our system and the file the contracts in the cabinets.

Soon after, I got accustomed to our product and I could pick up on certain calls as they were coming in. I received calls from customers both ready to book and still browsing around. I start booking some of the events. I would turn all calls in to my boss and she would turn them in to the general manager.

I didn't care about getting the credit because she was very cool. I knew she went to church often, but she didn't seem like the church folks I had encountered before. She and I became close friends. I soon realized that I had exaggerated how close we really were. She shared about a time when her pastor called for her and I remember talking to him like he trying to get some play. I said something like,

"Uh oh, Pastor trying to get some play." He was very cool and I could tell that I had crossed the line, but he remained cool.

I remember telling her about the phone call and she was not happy about it. Is this how pastors do it? They have their church, their wife, and their women on the side just like any other man, right?

Often she waited for the right time to tell the general manager that I was booking a lot of events while she was out of the office on sale calls. Because of this, he had her promote me to sales manager within months instead of two years. My salary almost tripled in one year.

CHAPTER 18
PRISON

Life was pretty good from the outside looking in. My girlfriend became pregnant. My boss embraced her as a friend. That was so huge to me. I've never seen anything like it.

Then, my first son is born! I knew I wanted to do right. I had a good job, very nice townhouse, a girl who I was convinced loved me, and we had a son. Based on what I've seen on television and my boss's encouragement, I was considering marriage. I thought it would solidify everything. I would then stop lusting after other girls, and I would have the strength now to say no to them when they throw themselves at me.

So, we were married on December 21, 2001. I was so looking forward to Christmas because I now had my first wife who favored my childhood crush, Aaliyah, and a new son! Nevertheless, having all this, my mind never changed from the fear of not having a main girl and some other girls on the side. This was what I had been taught my whole life. Deep down I wanted to stop. This girl has married me and we have a son! What's wrong with me?!

To my frustration, the girls I used to sneak around with me were still calling and offering themselves to me. I remember getting this call from this one girl who I was really weak for asking me to come over. I had only been married for two weeks! So in my logic, she was so fine and I wanted to go by and look at her, but wasn't going to do anything. So, I get one of the homies from the bar that was connected to the hotel to drive me over so I can have an excuse to leave just in case she tries something. I get there and my mind being enslaved to lust, I started to get weak. I told her I had to go and that my friend has to get back to work. On the way back to his Cadillac, I looked up to the sky and said in a very rude and disrespectful tone, "If you are real and you don't help me, this marriage won't last!"

The next day I was selling one of my cars to cut costs because I had a son. The guy that was trying to buy my car was trying to preach to me and invite me to church. Even though I prayed this rude prayer last night, I was totally blind to what was happening. I did not want to hear what he was saying, I just wanted the money for the car. He invited me to church with him. I told him I would think about it. I really was not planning on thinking about it.

CHAPTER 19
THE ENGAGEMENT

Back at work, my boss invited us to church again and I made a lot of excuses for not coming because of my experience as a young boy where I saw the preacher gamble, curse, and drink in front of me. I did not confess to her that I did not want anything to do with church because I thought she was cool, plus I didn't want to risk of ruining anything on my job. Nevertheless, after realizing there was an advantage coming up in the company, I thought to myself, *If she asks me again to go to church, I'm going to go ahead and go.* It seemed like as soon as I had this thought, she invited us within the next three days.

Sunday comes around and I was getting ready to go to church! I arrived at this place and everyone was so nice! Everyone was smiling. I knew it had to be fake! Then, the music started! It was high energy and it was making me feel good on the inside. I did not know what to think. The pastor came out wearing jeans and a sport coat coupled with swag. As he spoke, it scared me because it seemed like he was talking directly to me. He was calling out to me what seemed like all the stuff I was dealing with and how I was living. He was breaking it down--what the Bible called sin. The price that is owed for sin is death, not just the RIP that I used to hear growing up where after death, you are either sleeping in your grave or in the sky. That day, I was asking myself: the sky or the ground? I also remember him explaining what happens to people who continue to live this way without repenting and trusting in this Jesus for real forgiveness. I remember him explaining that Jesus was the Son of God. I had not heard that before! God had to come down and fix my mess. He does that in the form of His one and only begotten Son, Jesus. He loves us! He's calling us! His free gift of salvation is available today. He asked us who wanted to receive Christ that day. I so wanted to, but I was so afraid and ashamed, but I knew this was it. I thought, "Move Wayne, this is what you have been looking for your entire life." Yet, I couldn't move. It was so weird! It was like there was a force pressing against my chest. So, I didn't come forward and was so used to keeping my feelings to myself so I didn't tell anyone that I wanted to come forward. I just said, "I enjoyed it" and sped walked to my car.

The next week came and I went back to church and the same thing happened again. The third week came. The singing was good and the preaching was good again. After he gave a very quick and sharp word, he offered the invitation to come forward. It was like something invisible grabbed the back of my collar and carried me up to the altar with tears in my eyes. It was February 03, 2002 at 11:17 am. It was like a ton of bricks was lifted off my shoulders. My heart felt a gladness that I had never felt before. There was a level of excitement I was experiencing I couldn't wait to go tell my wife!

I arrived back at the house and began to snatch porn DVD's from under the couch and other hidden places in the house and throwing them outside in the dumpster. I began to take my bootleg CD's from my trunk and discard them into the dumpster. The message wasn't on pornography nor music, but somehow I just knew I needed to get rid of this stuff. I didn't want anything to interfere with what I was then experiencing!

CHAPTER 20
FIRST HUG

Even though I got saved, I didn't have a Bible. The next week, I went back to work at the hotel. It was my job to walk the lobby and speak to each guest to check on their stays. So, I walked over to this one man who was a white man with his Bible open on the table. I asked him, "How was your stay last night, sir?"

He said, "It was great!"

Then I invited him back to see us. I shared with him that I became a believer that week.

He closed his Bible and stood up and hugged me! When he did that, it was like a different set of weights fell from me. It felt like Jesus was hugging me! I never mentioned to him that I didn't have a Bible, yet he returned a few hours later with a brand new study Bible for me! Now, I didn't know where to start reading, so I just opened it. To my surprise, I opened it to Ephesians 6:19 which reads "As for me, that utterance may be given unto me, that I may boldly open my mouth, to make known the mystery of the Gospel." At that very moment, it was like those words jumped off the page and into my heart! Also, I knew for sure that the Lord wanted to use my mouth to bring Him glory.

I couldn't put the Bible down. It was like each time I opened the Bible, it was like the words on the pages were coming alive in my heart! I wanted to tell everyone about what I was experiencing. Jesus is the Son of God and He died for your sins. He wants to set you free. All you have to do is believe His Word! Believe everything He has said. He died but He came back to life for you! I was witnessing every opportunity!

It got to where over thirty people came to the Lord within the first month after my conversion. Every weekend, my truck was loaded with people I took to church. Everyone on the job was hearing about Jesus, everyone in the bar, my homies that I met in Montgomery, and the ones from my hometown. The atmosphere was already set anyway because my boss was carrying the light of Christ. We were now a team.

This new life was awesome. My church was awesome. My job was awesome. Soon after my conversion, my grandmother passed away. At the funeral, the lady that my grandmother had me speak to at church reveals to me that she was my grandmother. She says to me, "My son is your father, but he doesn't want to have anything to do with you, but I do. I'm not trying to make excuses for him but I would like to be in your life." I assured her that that would be fine. We began to talk about once or twice a week for about two years.

Meanwhile, the Lord had me bringing so many people to church that church leadership decided to propose that I become a deacon. I accepted this new role. I really wanted to be a servant leader like the deacon that Stephen revealed to us in the book of Acts, and also a better witness for Jesus.

I became interested in studying as many religions as I could to have conversations where I could handle objections and witness the truth of Jesus. I have bought resources to help deepen my knowledge in God and some other teachings that were pretty open in their stance against Christianity. I wanted to be equipped as I went out in the name of Jesus. God has opened doors where I'm teaching evangelism classes at my church, speaking at college universities, and even opened up with a Word before a city wide sold out play in Dothan, Alabama. Life seemed great.

CHAPTER 21
PRIDE INVASION

I began developing this mindset where I thought I knew everything. I had even developed this desire to remember scripture. It started off by trying to learn scripture to fight spiritually, but somewhere down the line, it seemed like it was for more knowledge. I began challenging everything. That mindset had then spilled over into my home and if I didn't see my wife studying like me, I thought she was not as devoted as I. She was not meeting my needs as much as I thought she should have. Since I was one of the deacons at my church, my phone was ringing off the hook day and night. I had to be there for people. I was dedicated. I was God's man. I was right there next to Stephen in the eyes of God.

I was preaching forgiveness and love to everyone else, yet was offended by how inconsiderate my wife was for not going out of her way to meet my needs. I did not talk to her on some days and this pattern continued.

Then one morning, I started my car for work and she started her car and she corners me in the kitchen and slowly says, "You're out here trying to save the world and don't even realize your wife is dying."

Oh my Lord, it felt like I was hit with a ton of bricks! I just grabbed her and held her. I made up in my mind at that moment on that day that I needed to repent! Also, after God restores me, I was going to cherish my wife through the grace of God that she was! Oh my God, what had pride done to me?!

With tears in my eyes, I asked her, "Sweetheart, I have been a mess. Haven't I?"

She responded in a meek, humble voice, "Yes, you have."

Starting that day, I read every scripture on pride in the Bible because the Lord revealed to me that it was my problem. I asked God to write all of them on the tablet of my heart. I wanted to know everything about pride according to God so that I would not fall back into this practice of sin. I shared this experience with my pastor and I sat down for a year to allow the Lord to heal me. I still was serving as a deacon, I just wasn't in a teaching capacity. In that year, the Lord was specifically healing me from pride. Youth of the church began gravitating toward me.

Finally, the Lord released me to teach again. I began to teach the teenagers and shared my testimony of how God brought me from darkness to light. I even shared how I fell into pride after receiving the Lord as my Savior within the first few years of walking with Him. The more I shared, the closer they gravitated. Sharing opened the door to discuss real issues they were facing in their lives. I was able to recommend relevant scriptures to them for their situations. The more I was able to pour into them, the more I realized what God wanted me to do. Yes, I was called to serve as a deacon, but I knew He wanted me to minister to the youth. He was revealing to me that everything He allowed to happen in my youth was a present for the present because most of my hurt and confusion happened in my youth.

CHAPTER 22
SEEKING GODLY WISDOM

About that time, God blessed us with another son. What a joy that was. I now had two sons! Wow, God! I had planned to be to them the exact opposite of what my father was to me. I did not want them to be treated how I was a child. I wanted to be who God wanted me to be to them. Even though my father wasn't present, it seemed like he was. So, I purposely spoke with the elder men at our church. We had a minister at our church in his eighties and a man in his seventies who was Chairman of the Deacon Board. I began to visit them and ask questions about manhood. They both had been walking with the Lord Jesus for over fifty years. These men always filled me with so much wisdom and love. Each principle they taught me always referred to the Bible.

On Wednesdays, it became routine to go to his house around four or four-thirty and have conversations until five forty-five. One of the first things they advised me was to stop focusing so much on what my father didn't do and start focusing on how God says to parent my own children. "Let the Bible be your gauge, son," they would tell me.

CHAPTER 23
GLIMPSE OF PURPOSE

A few years passed, and I became the general manager at a hotel here in the city. I even got to the point where I was set to run two hotels at the same time, but the pay wasn't right. I told the owner he needed to get another manager to help put finishing touches on the new hotel preparing to open here in downtown Montgomery.

During that time, we were in Tuscaloosa for the weekend visiting my sister. We were on our way to the store, and we passed a large high school. Out of nowhere, I had this thought and I expressed it out loud. The thought was that one day, the Lord was going to send me back to the schools.

My sister jokingly said, "Them folks aren't going to let you in those schools." At that time, she didn't know the Lord, so I knew she didn't understand, but that thought became very real to me, and I just kept it to myself.

CHAPTER 24
GOSPEL RAP!

I was well into serving as a deacon for about five years, and then I was introduced to Gospel rap. At first, I was hesitant because the first artist I heard was not good. It was positive, but it didn't sound good. So, I left that alone and later on heard this sermon of how it was from the devil anyway. Even though the message was more opinionated than scriptural, I didn't pay much attention to it because I didn't think that there was any good Gospel rap out anyway.

Then, there was another pastor friend whom I respected who asked me my opinion of Gospel rap. I told him that I didn't listen to it. He referred an artist to me by the name of Da T.R.U.T.H. I went and purchased the album. Surprisingly, when I put it on in the car, by the time I made it to track number three, I was blown away! It was principles! I was being helped! It was like worship for a hip hop head!

I immediately drove straight to my pastor's job. I gave him the CD and requested he listen to it on the way home. He called me on the way home and was just as blown away as me.

"Why don't we pray about a service based on this music," he said.

I said, "Yes sir!"

Lo and behold, two weeks later we had a spring break youth service and it was packed! In order to get the word out on the service, we went to juvenile centers, college campuses, and other churches and invited them out. Many youths responded to the call of Jesus that night. This was in March of 2008.

CHAPTER 25
YOUTH PASTOR

The next year, the youth pastor position became available at the church.

During my prayer time, I heard the Lord speak to my spirit that He wanted me to be the next youth pastor, but I didn't share it with anyone but my wife.

About a month or two later, we had a powerful Sunday service. My pastor told me after service that he needed to speak to me in my office for a few minutes before I left. I already had a strong feeling what it was about. I walked into his office and I sat down.

He asked, "Do you know why you're in here?"

I nodded. "Yes, sir."

"Congratulations, you're the new youth pastor." I could feel this weight leaving my body.

As the youth pastor, the Lord was allowing me to speak at youth revivals, camps, college campuses, assemblies, block parties, etc. Then, there was a tragic incident that happened here at a high school. Based on the unction of the Spirit, I went to the school and identified myself as a pastor and asks is there is anyway I could serve them. They allowed me to serve.

From that moment on, they opened the door for me to come serve before school started. The relationship with the school grew so much that I, accompanied by assistant principals and coaches, was able to take some boys to events off campus where they could learn good principles regarding manhood.

CHAPTER 26
THE CROSSROADS

My heart was bending more toward ministering to the young men than managing the hotel. Nevertheless, I persisted. There were times when the coaches would reach out and ask me to speak to some of the young men that were beginning to seem unreachable.

We were regularly having high energy youth services loaded with Christian rap music, mime dances, poetry, youth pastors speaking, games and activities for the purpose of reaching their culture. We wanted to be intentional with hosting small services for intimacy purposes all summer long with a plan of having one big service before school started back. I was starting to be torn between the opportunities that were pouring in to do ministry with the youth during the day and my career. I knew I wanted to honor the Lord in all that I was doing. It began to be a problem when I was using hotel time to go minister. I knew I was being challenged or commanded to let one go. I knew which one from the very first moment, but I wasn't ready to accept it. So, a few weeks went by and I tried to adjust some of the meetings until later in the evenings. Sometimes I wasn't successful in doing so. Then things just started happening on the job where it was becoming more evident what the Lord wanted me to do.

I knew something was going to have to give and I knew what it was. For a short moment, I was afraid to accept it. I knew the Lord was transitioning me out of the corporate world directly to minister on a broader scale. So, one day in the car, the Lord spoke to my spirit as clear as day. "Read Romans 6:11".

I had read Romans many times, but that scripture did not stand out as a familiar scripture. So, I reached back and grabbed my Bible off the back seat and I read it. That scripture read, "Likewise reckon ye also yourselves to be dead indeed unto sin, but alive unto God through Jesus Christ our Lord." Wow! I knew what He was telling me! Then, I heard in my spirit, "You have to die before you die, so you could live. I want you to start *Flat Line*."

All I knew was that it was going to have something to do with helping fatherless boys. Lately those were the ones He had been sending to me the most. I understood the pain, the rejection, the neglect, and the rebellion as an expression of neglect. I had to go and tell my wife about what transpired! "Lord help me!" I cried out.

CHAPTER 27
RADICAL OBEDIENCE

I prepared to go tell my wife what I'm sure the Lord had told me. Her response was so encouraging. She said, "I trust God and I trust that He speaks to you." Lord, talk about a Proverbs 31 wife!

Now at that time, she was a homemaker. By the end of the week, she had a job. To me, it was demonstrating that she wanted me to answer God's call on our lives. We agreed not to tell any of our family members off the bat. We wanted to allow God to show us more so we could better explain. I went and spoke to my pastor about it, and he said something that was encouraging as well. He said, "This is from God, but you have to be patient with people in getting this." As I began to meet with other leaders in sharing the vision, they were getting excited. Through God's grace, we linked up with some Gospel rappers and begin to do a few school assemblies, block parties, concerts, and church events.

I had taken a part-time, front desk clerk/auditor job at the hotel while doing some sales consulting on the side while waiting on the next move. I just wanted to be faithful. God's command of walking by faith and not by sight was the realest scripture in our lives at that moment.

During that time, my schedule had become flexible so I could move like I believed the Lord wanted me to. More fruit began to manifest and the harvest was more plentiful to me than ever before. Even though we were seeing godly fruit for days, the money was getting super tight and I didn't have any insurance. So, I prayed! "Lord, help us! You said in your Word that if a man can't take care of his family, he is worse than an unbeliever. Lord, I also believe You called me out here. I know that You wouldn't call me to do anything that contradicts who You are. So, please *help us* God!" I shouted.

A few days later, I was riding down the boulevard in Montgomery, and I heard the Lord say to call Bob. I hadn't spoken to my friend Bob in a few months. So, I obeyed. After small talk, there was a weird silence. I then said, "Listen bro, I don't know why, but the Lord told me to call you."

He responded with, "I know why. It's because Joe and I were talking about you yesterday saying whether or not we thought you'd ever consider being a bus driver?" Immediately, I knew this was the Lord. One, that job has the best insurance in the city, I will be right smack in the middle of their culture, and I would be off on the weekends and the summers…this would be perfect!

The only thing was passing the state exam and naming all the parts on a school bus!

"Okay, Lord!" I said. "You know I had no man to teach me anything mechanical." As I prayed and sought council, I knew I had to walk by faith on this one, too. So the next day, I went to Troy highway to find out what it would take to apply for a the position.

They told me that I needed to get a study book from the driver's license office.

I did and I studied intensely. Then, it was time for me to go take the written test. I passed the basic part the first time, but it took me a few times to pass the written brake test. After I passed that test, I had to name over sixty parts on a school bus in front of a state representative. I studied the manual as well as watched hours of footage on YouTube about parts on a school bus. The time came for me to take the test and I got an "A" on the test.

CHAPTER 28
DIVINE PROMOTION

Summer was coming up and my nephew who lived in Linden was planning on coming back up to Montgomery for our big back-to-school youth event. The year prior, he gave his life to Christ at our youth service. He was excited to be picked up to return this year. He played a vital role being a vessel and exalting God in the ministry.

Remember my grandmother that was confirmed at my other grandmother's funeral? Someone from their family called me a few months earlier and invited me to their family reunion this summer. They made me aware that my father was going to be there, and he didn't know I was coming. I knew I didn't want to go.

"I'll pray about it," I said. *Please God, don't make me go!* __

Months pass and it was the Saturday morning of the reunion and a week before our big youth event. On this morning, my wife and I planned to hang out that day. I was in the bathroom getting ready, and I heard the dreadful words in my spirit, "I want you to go to that reunion."

"No, God! Please! I don't want to go!" *Hey, maybe my wife won't want to go.*

As I entered the living room, I said, "Sweetie, God just told me He wants me to go to that reunion."

She looked at me and smiled. "Amen. If God is telling you to go, then you should go."

I went and while on the way, I called my nephew and told him I was coming to pick him up because I was still disciplining him. So, I had to go to Linden to pick him up and then go to the reunion which is held about seven to ten minutes outside of Linden. We get to the reunion and as soon as I walked in, I saw this guy who looks like me twenty years ago. I mingled with people I knew and within about twenty minutes, one of his relatives comes over and whispers in my ear, "Hey, let's not do this now. He will call you."

Hearing those words in my ear sent fire through my body! I was fire mad! Now, I know that the Word says that sin crouches at your door and desires to have you, but you must rule over it. I didn't rule over it. I was so ready to get in the car to tell my wife, "See. I told you. This is why I didn't want to come here!" I hadn't dealt with the anger that I thought subsided, so sin bit me! I began to lie. I told my nephew that I had to get back to Montgomery because I had something to do even though we had just arrived.

We were on our way back to my Linden so I could drop him off and he said to me, "Unc, please don't forget to come get me next week."

I was still dealing with what just happened twenty minutes ago, and he was clueless about it. I didn't want him to be affected by it, so I said what I thought sounded good at the time. I responded, "I won't."

Then he said, "Unc, I wish the whole football team could experience what I experience when I come to Montgomery. Church is different up there."

I respond with an answer, but my mind was still on what just happened. Yet, I still said, "Ask your coach."

It was a Saturday afternoon around four o'clock. His coach didn't live in Linden. He lived about twenty minutes away. Right after I tell him to ask his coach, my nephew said, "There he go right there, Unc!"

In my mind, I'm like, "Oh Lord. C'mon!" Nevertheless, I pull into the barbershop where he was. The barbershop was packed. So, I walked in and said, "Hey Coach, I'm"

He cuts me off while giving me this 'why are you bothering me look,' and said, "I know who you are."

Now, because I still haven't dealt with what happened twenty minutes ago, I could barely look him in the eye. I was fumbling big time! I began to speak by saying… "Ahh evvvery yearrrrr.. in Monntt……" I then turned to my nephew and said, "I'm going to let my nephew tell you!"

Then my nephew nervously said, "It be good."

I told him to tell him how it's good and how he was affected when he attended. To this day, his answer changed the course of my life.

He then responded with confidence, "Well, when I go to the youth events at my uncle's church, I understand the Word clearer. It's broken down to our level plus, while there, I realize that I need to take the Word more seriously and live out what I'm learning by being more responsible to Christ and to others."

At that moment, Coach turned to me, pointed and said, "We will be there!" I took off running and said, "It's this Saturday."

He said, "I know!"

I took off running again and came back and I said, "It's in Montgomery."

He said, "I know!"

I took off running again and while making my third round around the shop, he said, "The cheerleaders will be there too!"

I walked back to the car blown away! By the time I got in the car, the Lord was revealing to me why He really had me come to Linden on that day and that particular time. Everything was divine from the time I picked up my nephew to the point at the reunion where those disappointing words were whispered in my ear. It was all God! I could not wait to call and tell my wife the good news! I told her about what happened at the reunion, but it was small potatoes compared to what my heavenly Father had done. I was rejected by my earthly father and promoted by my heavenly Father. I ended up not leaving early like I had said and did my normal hangout on the block with the guys I used to run with. Just like most visits, I normally showed my face in the hangout spots while checking up on everyone. When they asked me what I'd been up to, I was able to tell them about ministry.

They loved hearing it. Sometimes, it would open the door to discuss the Gospel in the presence of two to fifteen guys at a time, some females. Sometimes, they were the females I used to take advantage of. As I was testifying, I was apologizing at the same time.

Some of the ladies would say, "You don't have to apologize."

I would respond, "Yes I do because I took something from you that I didn't deserve because I had not made a lifetime commitment to you."

Sometimes it was convicting to them because they most likely allowing a man to take advantage of them at that moment. That night was one of the best witnessing nights I have ever had in Linden. It was so on fire that some of the guys on the block said that they were going to come to the event. They were saying things like, "Wayne, we see you on Facebook. You're doing good things in Montgomery. We need something like that down here."

I said, "Man, I am praying for y'all and I wish I could be here more, but God could be calling some of you to be used by God to spark a revival here." That night, I think I gave out about ten Bibles because I kept a box of Apologetics Bibles with me at all times.

The following Saturday came and the guys on the block that said they were coming didn't show up, but Coach Williams and his boys and the cheerleaders rolled up on a bus. It was liberating to see them get off of that bus. This was my hometown football team in Montgomery at our youth event. It made my heart so happy! I felt like I was honoring the Lord by reaching out to my Jerusalem.

The service started. We kicked it off with a prayer! Then, we explained to them that this is a service that God has set up for them. We shared that everything that will happen on that night, will be intentionally done by the Lord to engage them! Then, we brought out our Youth Mass Community Choir. Then, the youth mime team danced. Then, poetry was read. Next, we had our first Gospel rap group. After, we had a youth pastor speak for 10 minutes followed by another Gospel rap group and a comedian. Then, we had a young lady from a local college give her testimony followed by another Gospel rap group. Then, we had an Apologist speak on how you can know for sure that God is real. It was a three-hour service and the boys and cheerleaders were engaged the entire service. Many testimonies were given from them that night.

Around 1 am, I receive a call from Coach. He said, "I apologize for calling you so late, but I have never in my life seen young people that engaged when it came to the Gospel." He said the boys and the girls have been talking about what they learned and gained from this experience the entire ride back to Linden and how they are going to start living for God.

Now, what I did not know about Coach was that he was

on the Board that connected him to many coaches here in the city. He reached out to many coaches at the beginning of the week about his experience at our youth event. He told them that he was the only one there with his team even though it was packed. He said, "Your boys need to be connected with this guy."

Right after that, some coaches contacted me, but some he wanted me to contact myself. At that moment, God took the ministry and spread it all over the city. We were doing an assembly almost every week. I was invited to do many devotions for the teams here in the city. Also, I began to travel home more and become more involved with Linden football team.

So much was happening! God began opening doors for me to go and minister at detention centers. That was a big deal for me. It was really easy for me to relate to those guys because I knew how easily I could have been in the same exact position they were in. I tried to be very careful as I gave my testimony and street knowledge of how God graced me out. I really wanted to make the point to them that I wasn't the rule, but the exception to the rule. I explained to them that I believe the Lord saved me because of His sovereignty. He knew I was going to say yes to His call.

I shared, "He knew I was going to come here with you all and share His good news because He loves you all so much. He wants to save and use you all right now. As long as you have a pulse, you have a chance."

God was moving so strongly that they would open up the chapel for one Sunday out of each month for me to go over and preach to fifty to sixty boys at a time. They were from all over Alabama.

The word got back to people in the community that God was using me. I was getting offers to come onto television programs, radio broadcasts, podcasts, and many Sunday school invites all over the city.

CHAPTER 29
ROBOCOP

The next summer rolled around and the buzz was out about our big summer event. The last event we had at our church was standing room only. During that year, we developed relationships with more coaches and principals, so we figured it was going to exceed the room of the church.

During prayer one day, I believed the Lord wanted to have the next event downtown. Getting space downtown is expensive. Nevertheless, I would use some of my old hotel contacts to get a discount for the event. I went to visit the hotel where I thought I would get the discount, but the employees I knew a few years back weren't there anymore. The hotel staff quoted a ridiculous amount just for the space. The newest, largest hotel in the city was downtown as well, but I knew for sure I wasn't going to have any luck there. As I was walking back to my car talking to the Lord, I said, "Lord, I was sure you wanted to have it down here."

As I am touching the handle on my car, I get tapped on my shoulders. "Dewayne, what are you up to? What you doing down here?"

I hadn't seen this fella in years. I preached at his church's youth revival a few years back, so I knew he was a believer. I told him that I was trying to find space for another youth event for the summer. He instructed me to go across the street. He told me where to go and said, "Tell them I sent you."

Again, I wasn't going there because I just knew they were out of my budget even though I didn't have one! By faith, I locked my car, put another quarter in the meter, and walked across the street. I asked to speak to a sales representative that could assist me with event space.

A very professional man came down and began to ask me questions as we headed over to the meeting rooms. "What are you planning?" he asked.

I told him and he didn't seem excited about what I was saying. Then, I said, "Oh by the way, Jarred told me to tell you he sent me." Everything changed at that moment. He quoted a price that was 75% less than the old hotel I went to a few minutes ago. His price included set up and breakdown with a huge stage. I was elated! I quickly told some brothers from Frazer Men's Ministry who were very supportive of the work of *Flat Line* here in the city. I asked them for the money so I could quickly pay for this and get a contract. They gave me the funds and I secured a contract.

The date for the event finally came. There were nearly four hundred people there. There were teams, cheerleaders, youth groups, Frazer United Methodist Men as chaperones, principals, etc. There were black, white, green, and yellow folks there that night celebrating Jesus! We had all the ingredients like the previous events, just on a larger scale. After all the entertainment, I preached a message about Robocop. God used the example of how someone else was behind the scene controlling him and when they wanted to shut him down they did even though he thought he was in control. That's how the devil is handling anyone in this room that has not confessed Jesus as their Lord and Savior. That night 47 youth got saved! Linden football team was at that event too along with others as well. I mentioned them because they drove the furthest and had to get hotel rooms. I got up that morning and went and ate breakfast with them along with some of the artists that was involved in the event. We made sure all of them had some music before they left.

After that, a core group was formed. We were made up of a mime team, a singing group, two rap groups, and a preacher. Over the course of two years, we went on to do over fifty events all over the United States. Everyone was calling, it didn't matter whom. If you would have let us come with the Gospel, we were down to roll. We had given out over a thousand study Bibles. The ministry was reaching far outside just concerts, school assemblies, block parties. We were having regular Bible studies on Thursdays where high school athletes are showing up. We were seeing young men turn from the wannabe gangster lifestyle to sold-out believers. We had the *Flat Line* gear and it was spreading in the schools. God was showing us more and more of His plan for *Flat Line* as we developed the high school AAU basketball team called *Flat Line* Ballerz. AAU basketball can get expensive, so we went and found sponsors for the boys. We would have regular Bible studies with guys at least twice a month. The boys were from four different high schools here in the city. It was intentional because we knew here in Montgomery, the West was beefing with the North ("Nawf"). So, to have these guys on the same team and have studies with them was all God.

CHAPTER 30
AFRICA

The Lord opened a door for me to travel to Ghana, on the continent of Africa, to preach a youth retreat. So much was gained from that trip. Now, looking back, I would have done some things differently. I thank God that the two ladies I ended up staying with were godly women. Even in the States, I would not have put myself in a position like that where it could possibly look like something could happen. Don't get me wrong, there were no hints of immorality in these ladies. I'm just a man and a preacher and those are ways that the Lord has shown me to guard my heart and abstain from the very appearance of evil.

But, the experience was life-changing. The hospitality could not have been any better. I went over to serve and sacrifice, but it felt like a luxury vacation. I got to pray for so many officials while there. Many times, I wondered if I was worthy. Nevertheless, they just had a high respect for ministers of the Gospel. Compared to the way we live here, you would think they would complain.

Purposefully, for ten days, I was trying to see and hear

if someone would complain, and there was not one complaint. One night we were sitting in the living room of the house that they had put me up in and I saw a Coke commercial and jokingly said, "Man, I could use a Coke right now." Now the commercial wasn't in English, but I recognized the Coke. It had gotten to a point where if I mentioned something, they would get it. So, I noticed one of the young ladies had stood up. I thought she had gone to her room to go to sleep because it was around 10 pm. It turned out, she had walked up to a spot where they sell Cokes to get me a Coke. It was not a short walk. I was like, "Oh my Lord!"

From then on, I watched what I said because of their overwhelming love for Jesus and service. It was very convicting. Another thing that encouraged me was the night that I was scheduled to preach. It was raining. We didn't know how many were going to show up because most of them were going to have to walk. We prayed for hours that God would bring the harvest. Lo and behold, over 150 people showed up that night. The students encouraged me so much with what they learned. It was an experience. I was coached on speaking slowly so everyone could understand because many were not fluent in English.

It was one of the best nights of my life. Oh my goodness, the worship band! One time, it was about fifty of them jumping around chanting something! All I saw were tears and crying out! I asked my chaperone what they were saying.

She said they were chanting, "God, we want to serve you in our youth!"

Oh, my! I began to shout and yell praises unto God!! Hallelujah!! That experience was recorded on social media and while I was in Africa, my inbox was blowing up where I was receiving invites to come speak at youth services and camps! It was amazing. I stayed there for ten days, but at the close of my trip, was asked to stay a month. I had to get back because the day I was to fly back in, I was scheduled to speak at a youth event downtown that night at six pm.

CHAPTER 31
PORSCHA

We were still doing music (concerts, block parties, church events, etc.) for *Flat Line* also on a pretty frequent basis. In *Flat Line*, we only had one female rapper. Not intentionally, she was just the only one. Her name was Porscha. She was a dope MC, but more than that, in my eyes, she was a female Paul. She was so passionate about evangelism. She would even open her house for us to bring in athletes. She would cook and go down the hall and pray while we have studies. She traveled overseas a lot for missions and I knew where she kept her key as well as her security code to her house just in case we needed a quiet spot that week for the Bible study.

She kept the balance in the ministry so that we wouldn't get lost in success. She constantly reminded us why we were doing what we were doing. She was single, but I respected her more when she pulled me to the side and told me that I was too busy in ministry.

I listened. I said, "Explain more."

She said that if I am so busy out here and not intentionally blocking off time for my family that it was going to blow up in my face. Her talk hit me like a ton of bricks. From that point on, I purposely took off July and was not accepting any outreach events that month. It was all about my family. I think we had this conversation in May and she called or texted me every day to make sure I hadn't accepted any events. They were calling frequently. One was a city-wide event, but as they were explaining what it was, I could hear Porscha's voice in my head. To this day, I am still doing as she told me.

There was this call that I received around two in the morning that she had passed and not only did she pass, but she was murdered. The alleged murderer had just spent the previous weekend with us in Atlanta. My heart dropped! I was praying this was a nightmare and I was going to wake up to reality. Nevertheless, it wasn't a nightmare, it really happened. That hit the ministry's family and the entire community very hard.

CHAPTER 32
THE UPROOT

I had a few churches express their interest in me as senior pastor, associate pastor, and youth pastor. I was like, "Lord, whatever you want." I

I shared with Pastor Willis R. Walker of Anointed Warrior Hill, my pastor, about the opportunities. He said he would be praying that if I move, I move where God wants me to be. He stated that I had served there for fourteen years and if God was moving me, I had his blessing.

That was so encouraging to me. So, I went on a fast in July so that I could hear clearly for such a huge decision.

This process started in June 2016 and I didn't get a clear answer from the Lord until November of 2016. After meeting with some local pastors and visiting various churches, I knew in my spirit that Strong Tower at Washington Park was the perfect fit for me. The Lord showed me why. The church was in the neighborhood where most of the young men I mentored lived. Some of them could walk to the services and events. As I studied their ministry's philosophy, it reminded me of the book of

Acts. I loved the community missionary concept. I loved the vision of being part of a church that was open weekly to impact the community in better ways than would be able to minister as one person. This is where I believed the Lord was guiding me.

Remember Porsha. She was the main one praying and hoping and encouraging me to come on staff at Strong Tower. The night of the vote, she was the first one there with her *Flat Line* shirt on. I remember being slightly embarrassed, but honored by her. Pastor Terrence let everyone know what they were thinking and wanted to present me to the church for prayer.

They asked if anyone wanted to testify about me and my life and before he could finish, she jumped up and said, "I do!"

She gave the most beautiful testimony you could ever give. She never got to see me on earth, get the position but I know she sees the work manifesting.

Meanwhile, the boys had gone to their coach and shared about our Bible studies and how they hang out at our house and learn about life. With this information making it back to the head coach, I became the chaplain for the Carver High School football team and trained some other ministers on chaplain work at various schools.

Along with the chaplain position, I was the youth pastor at Strong Tower at Washington Park. Right off the bat, Pastor Terrence, Lead Pastor at Strong Tower, was determined to reach out to supporters for support. The school bus ministry was powerful so the demand became larger. He set up a meeting with a state organization that would have paid me to develop ministries on college campuses here in Montgomery. I knew my heart was with the fatherless high school boys. Nevertheless, I did college ministry before. I asked if they would give me a few weeks to pray on it. The Friday before I was going to meet with them, the Lord began to make it clearer than ever what His plan was for me. I was still working part-time at the hotel. Working there was such a huge blessing because when I travel as a family, I got a really good discount.

I was getting ready to walk out the door to head to work for my 2pm shift. Around 1:45 the blinds opened to the backyard and I saw this long black snake slithering across the yard. At that moment, I didn't have a gun, hoe, or shovel. I felt helpless, but it was too late to call in. I asked my wife and children not to go outside and that I would handle it when I returned home. I didn't know what I was saying. It was going to be dark when I got home! So, I just went ahead to work. I clocked in and could not get that image out of my head. Finally, after about twenty minutes, I asked the general manager if I could get someone to cover my shift because I had an emergency at home.

He worked it out and by 2:45 pm, I went to try to buy a shot gun, but because my address differed from my license, I had to wait a few days. So, I left there and went to Lowe's to look for a hoe or a shovel. On the way there, I received a call from one of the players from Carver High School. He said, "What's up, Mr. Dewayne? What's the move today?" I said, "There is no move, I need to go home and cut my grass because I saw a snake about an hour ago. I'm headed to buy a shovel or a hoe now." To my complete shock, he replied, "What if we come over and cut the grass and rake the leaves, will you do a Bible study?" I said in an overwhelming voice, "Sure." At that time, it was a twenty minute drive to my house from where they were. So, I was running around trying to get tools and snake stuff so it took me about forty-five minutes to get home.

To my surprise, I pulled up to the house and it was about eight players working on the yard. They had everything from weed eaters to lawn mowers. Some had gotten their uncle's equipment and some were on our equipment. My eyes were full of tears. This was a Friday evening!

I tried to help, but they wouldn't let me.

They said, "We got it." Since they were so busy, I went to the store to get us some chicken and Gatorade. After they finished, we had our Bible study. It lasted until 9 pm that night.

Saturday rolled around and I received a call from a high school basketball coach. He said that the boys asked if I could come out after practice on Sunday and give a quick Word.

I said, "Yes, and Lord I hear you." I went, and it was powerful. I received text messages from the players on Sunday night after the study. I knew that the Lord wanted me to stay focused with the young men that were in high school because that's where the real internal and external trauma happened in my life.

Monday rolled around. I went back to the organization and testified of the previous weekend and all the signs that God was showing me. The Lord knew we needed the money, but I knew it wasn't His will for us at that time.

They were so receptive that one of the guys had tears in his eyes and he said he knew what I was passing up. He also said, "I have more respect for you now than I did when I first met you. I know it's not about money with you."

We just hit the ground running again. Mentoring with *Flat Line* had an intentional focus on high school young men. We began having two-hour Apologetics Bible study every Thursday. We would have anywhere from two to fifteen guys show up for the studies. We would feed the guys first mimicking how Jesus did. He served and then He taught.

There were testimonies of guys going from straight F students to then C and B students. There were also testimonies from boys who were filled with anger, like I was, but now filled with the love of Jesus. Administrators stopped us to tell us about certain students who used to terrorize and bully others but changed to walking around with their Bibles trying to preach to everyone. Praise God for that because we were intentional about teaching discipleship according to the Scriptures. We also taught a lot on witnessing and loving your neighbor as yourself.

We have started a bi-monthly evening youth service called "iENGauge." iENGauge is derived from Acts 17:16-

34 where Paul engaged the secular culture without compromising the Gospel. There is a symbolic meaning behind the spelling of the name. The 'I' is lowercase because we are the small beings engaging people, but it's actually by God's power we are able to engage. "Gauge" is spelled the way it is because the Word of God has to be the gauge. Of course, the way it is pronounced stems from God's children being guided.

During our services, we are intentional when it comes to being divinely balanced with fun and Word. We have pizza and juice, table games, Bible games, worship & arts, DJ, Gospel rap, live videos, Word, and Q & A.

- This divine opportunity is available to me with the Montgomery Baptist Association who has partnered with sixty-one churches here in our River Region. I have been hired as a Ministry Resident to serve our churches and assist in them partnering with our schools. I serve as a counselor, a consultant, a connector, and a coordinator.

There are so many ways that we as a church can partner with our schools.

- School supplies drive, nonperishable food backpack programs, school uniform/clothing closet, or annual drives for other unmet needs.

- Landscaping and beautification projects are ideal for families with children who want to be involved.

- Sponsor a Boy Scout or Girl Scout Troop, a chess, crocheting, or knitting club by providing troop and activities leaders.

- Adopt a school to provide workshops, seminars and conferences on self-esteem, bullying, actions, consequences and choices.

- Create a team that participates in every school board meeting. Your presence at meetings, even without bringing forward issues, will communicate to the decision makers that your church cares about the education of children.

- Sponsor a community-wide clean-up day during the fall and spring semester.

- Ask teachers to post individual classroom needs on Donors Choose, and then ask church members to help fund things that will go directly to the classroom.

- Support a tutoring program during an after-school time at the school, church or other neighborhood facilities.

- Encourage them to spread the good news about the great things happening in public schools.

- Schools are often lacking volunteers for events. Meet with the principal early in the fall and find out which events need additional manpower.

- Have the church cover any expenses for background checks or medical tests related to volunteering in schools. Sometimes the smallest obstacle becomes the biggest excuse!

- Once a month, provide treats to the school staff. Every school has a teachers' work area and every employee of the school will appreciate if you provide bagels, donuts or a healthy lunch snack.

- Spending on arts and music is extremely limited. Utilize church talent to organize a choir, present one-day workshops, after school, or any opportunity for children to get exposure to art and music.

- Find out what projects are important at a school and help provide the supplies. If they have a garden, make sure they have tools. If they are allowing children to paint murals, make sure they have the paint they want.

- Church members "adopt" classrooms or schools and pray for them, provide inexpensive, necessary school supplies and surprise them with appreciation gifts.

- Mentoring: Church members serve as "lunch buddies" who meet weekly with students to listen, share and play games or a daily presence from a male(s) assisting teachers during morning/afternoon duty and monthly mentoring parties for improvement or other positive behavior awards.

- Chaplain work

- Pre-game breakfasts

- Pre-game meal

Now, as great as these activities are, if you are a true believer, you know the real problem resonates in the heart. Sin is the ultimate problem. Yes. Even after we explain that we don't deal with Satan's discipleship mechanism, we still will have on our hands a tougher battle. This is why we must engage.

Satan has weaponized music and entertainment in our culture today and the church for the most part doesn't seem to have an effective answer for it. With this generation, you can't only say to them to not listen to that music because it's promoting sin. That's not enough for them. One, they want to know why. Two, what shall we listen to then? Your music? This is especially the case in the urban culture or where that teenager or the young adult is used to rap music.

We have to engage them the way Jesus engaged people and/or the way Paul engaged people in Athens in Acts 17:16-34. If you examine this text, you will see how Paul even quoted their paganism to engage them without compromising the Gospel.

Another example, which is my favorite one, is found in John 4:7-26. There is an account of Jesus engaging a woman at the well in the hottest part of the day. Nevertheless, if you look closely, you could see so many things in his engagement.

For me, there are four principles that I gained from this

and I use it when I preach and/or witness. First, He met her on common ground by discussing something that He knew she could understand naturally. He did this by asking her for some water. Secondly, He then swung the conversation over to the spirit realm by letting her know that if she really knew who was asking for this water, she would be asking Him for living water. She replied, "Sir tell me where to get some of that! I wouldn't need this old well." Thirdly, He then used His Word to bring conviction by asking her to "go call your husband." Now, of course, He's God so He knew she didn't have a husband, but He was setting her up for the Word to expose her true condition to herself. Her response was, "I don't have a husband." Jesus says, "You're right. You've been married five times and the guy you're shacking with now is not your husband." She's convicted and ready for Jesus (The Messiah) now. Lastly, He gives her what she's longing for and she proves it by saying right after her conviction, "I know the Messiah will tell us all things when He comes." Jesus said, "That's me, the one you're speaking to now."

Now, check this out. The Bible said the same woman that was filled with all this shame and guilt went back telling everyone, come you got to see this man that knows everything about me. Only God can know everything about you.

Based on observation of the church as a whole, we've been missing the first principle for sure. Some have been missing the second and went straight for the law (don't do this, don't say this, don't go here, don't wear this) or some have skipped all three principles and went straight for Jesus loves you. Jesus didn't skip those principles. In the urban context, our children are the only ones who have to give up their music when they get saved according to most Black rural or urban pastors. In other contexts, if that youth was into secular country music, getting drunk and having sex, their youth pastor would direct them to country Christian music. Same thing in contemporary pop, their youth pastor would direct them to Christian Contemporary music. Most of our Black teens are into hip-hop or rap. As soon as one of them decides to repent of their sins and live for God, they are persuaded to listen to Gospel music that sounds nothing like the sound they have grown to love. The sound isn't evil. The beats aren't evil. The content that was coming through the air waves by the prince of the air was what was evil. A major problem that must be addressed with predominantly Black churches is the lack of youth pastors. Sadly, most Black youth do not get engaged in a way that truly helps them be disciplined. I am not trying to make a case for rap. Rap isn't what saves a person. Nevertheless, it can be used as a discipleship tool for young people already in love with it. R.A.P. in itself is not evil. The word RAP stands for rhyme and poetry. If you look at the Book of Psalms, Book of Proverbs, Song of Solomon, Book of Job, Book of Ecclesiastes, all these are poetic books and there are rhymes in the book of Psalms. So, beats are not evil, men's hearts are. We take culture from our Black youth instead of engaging that culture. Not just with music, but dance, poetry, and the arts. Who's going to talk to our Black youth in church about the temptations they are facing on Snapchat and Instagram when you don't even know what they are. Most of our older Black pastors couldn't tell you what the word 'T.H.O.T' means or what it means to "pain" a girl. You can't effectively minister if you can't communicate. Why aren't most of our Black teens coming to seek council from most of our Black pastors? One, they don't think we care enough to even try to understand their world. If you won't even try to understand their world, their mindset changes. They don't feel valued and since you don't value them, they don't value the church. Their mindset is also to go as long as they have to, but as soon as they leave the house and that boring church, they are done with church. Check the statistics of the percentile of youth that abandons their faith after high school to see if I'm lying.

When we fail to engage our youth and their culture with the Bible being the gauge, then we basically just hand them over to the devil. For black folks, we are very passionate and defensive about how bad we were treated during slavery. By right, we should be. But for my leaders, when we fail to properly engage our youth with truth and grace, we leave them to their slave master. The Bible tells us in John 8:44 that the devil has children. He abuses his children. He is the father of lies and he has been a murderer from the beginning. In John 10:10, the Bible says, He [Satan] comes to kill, steal, and destroy. He is a deceiver." 2 Corinthians 11:14 says that "he disguises himself as an angel of light." He is too much for our young people to fight without proper information.

Why am I on this music so much? Well, the Bible says Satan is here roaming the earth. He got kicked out and lost his position in heaven, but the Bible never said that he lost his ability to make music. So, if he's here and he is a musician and I can't see him, I am going to look for him there first. Ezekiel 28:13 describes his workmanship in heaven. It reads, "The workmanship of your timbrels and pipes was prepared for you on the day you were created." Now, I know some still argue that this verse doesn't mean that he was a worship leader. The Hebrew text of this verse has been difficult to interpret. Isaiah 14 is another point of reference to look into. I personally believe he was based on my study. This is why. The Bible says in Romans chapter 8, verse 6 that "to be carnally minded is death; but to be spiritually minded is life and peace." He also says in Isaiah 5:20, "Woe unto those that call good evil and evil good." Satan knows the Bible better than you and I.

I have seen firsthand the power and influence of music, doesn't matter the genre. There are some teens that will lose their mind over music. The Bible tells us also in Ephesians to watch out for the schemes of the devil.

He is keeping a lot our youth in slavery and getting them to celebrate their bondage and destruction. For example, in hip hop they call cars "whips" and they are always glorifying chains, and they call young ladies "hoes." Tell me that isn't slavery (whips, chains, hoes). Then, the most popular music out now is "trap" music. The goal is to be on a rat race, getting that cheddar, to be the best trap boy. Now look at this spiritually. If I am on a rat race, that means I am a rat. What kind of cheese do you put on a trap when you want to kill a rat? Cheddar!

There's more! Jesus said that He is the bread of life and that we shouldn't worship anyone besides Him. He is a triune God so that include The Father and the Holy Ghost. Now, in hip-hop/urban culture, all focus is on chasing the bag. The bag is money. Worship money! But check this out, money is sometimes called bread.

Now, let's be clear. Satan hadn't just come on the scene with his music in hip-hop and "trap" music. He's been publically working through jazz and blues all the way back to 1900's before the so-called "Devil's Music" would find its true cultural footing. Then, the rock and roll, then the hip-hop era, and now the biggest genre or the one that is affecting our youth the most is this "trap" music era.

Romans 6:11 commands that we must consider ourselves dead to sin and alive to God in Christ Jesus. Let's die to our old way of thinking because sometimes it could lead to neglect, which is sin. Let's come alive to God in Christ Jesus and go like He commanded us before He ascended back into Heaven.

I pray that we would be a people that will be intentional in effectively engaging our young people in culture without compromising God's Gospel. I pray that we would pay attention to those around us who are obviously troubled, but also to those who appear to be alright, but you know that their home life/family life is off a lot. Those people are hurting and are waiting on you to bring Jesus to them. How do I know this? Because I lived it! God engaged me through His people and I finally knew this was right! God helped me to overcome all of my hurt. He then helped me to overcome all of my neglect. He then helped me to overcome all of my insecurities. He then helped me to overcome all of my fears. He uses people like you. Will you be willing to be used by God to "flat line" to sin and engage this culture with the Word of God being the one and only true gauge?

Blessings!

GEORGE WASHINGTON CARVER
2017 FOOTBALL SEASON

DEWAYNE REMBERT

THE MONTGOMERY BAPTIST

MONTGOMERY
Baptist Association

A WEEKLY NEWSLETTER

Serving Christ Through Montgomery Area Churches

NEAL HUGHES, DIRECTOR OF MISSIONS • THURSDAY, FEBRUARY 15, 2018

FROM REBEL TO REDEEMED

I have fond memories of going to church as a young boy with my grandmother. I remember her giving me candy and going to sleep in her lap during the sermon. When I was eleven or twelve years old, my cousin and I started sneaking out of the services to listen to Master P, Tupac, and Juvenile in his mother's car in the church parking lot. My grandmother began suffering from dementia and eventually stopped attending church because of the disease. Before long, I quit going to church and my life was all about hip hop music and the philosophy that it portrayed.

Dewayne Rembert
Ministry Resident

When I was sixteen years old, I was at a local gambling/shot house in my neighborhood on a Sunday afternoon when a well-known preacher walked in, sat down at the card table with his Sunday suit on, and began drinking and gambling. Despite not being a follower of Jesus at that time in my life, I knew something was very wrong with what he was doing. Moreover, my most vivid memory of church at that time was a lady telling me, "Get those earrings out of your car and pull your pants up, or you're going to hell." It was that day that I knew that I didn't want anything to do with church. I was angry and confused about the whole church thing and wished that I had someone with whom to

discuss this situation, but I kept it to myself. The fact that I had no father to talk to about the confusing image that this so-called preacher was modeling of God became a focus of my young life and eventually made me become very angry with life in general.

From the time I was sixteen until I became twenty-six years of age I lived an immoral life filled with rebellion and anger. Thanks to God, the Holy Spirit, and Jesus, I heard the gospel for the very first time on February 3, 2002 at 11:17 am. I eventually became a youth pastor (in 2009) and in 2012 started an outreach ministry called Flatline Movement. This ministry is derived from Romans 6:11 which says, "Likewise you also, reckon yourselves to be dead indeed to sin, but alive to God in Christ Jesus our Lord." The focus of this ministry is to encourage all, specifically young people, to "die" before they die so they can live! It's designed by God to engage our young culture without compromising the gospel. We do that through music, discipleship, and sports.

As a ministry resident with Montgomery Baptist Association, I look forward to partnering with our churches and pastors in taking the gospel to our schools. God is at work in the hearts of our young people! Please pray for me and for Flatline, and to free to reach me at drember@mgmbaptists.org for more information on how you can help your church reach the youth of what God is doing.

~Dewayne Rembert

Co-vocational Pastors Breakfast

RALLY
for the

You Don't Know Who'll Need Those Socks!
Sock It To Me!

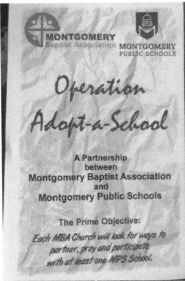

ABOUT THE AUTHOR

Dewayne Rembert grew up in Linden, Alabama. He has been married to his best friend Leslie for sixteen years and they have three wonderful children, Devin 16, Dorian 13, and Journi 6. There were good times in his life but deep down inside he felt the pain and rejection of being raised in the absence of a father. His grandmother became his guardian because at that time his mother was not really involved in his life. Despite seeing himself as "not good enough" during the days of his youth, he somehow was able to move up the corporate ladder in a well-respected hotel chain after graduating from high school. He heard the Gospel for the first time on February 3, 2002, at 11:17 A.M. and his life was never the same again. Later he became the General Manager of the hotel.

He served as a deacon for seven years at his church and during that time of service, he was stirred with a passion to reach young people for Christ. This passion to share the Gospel with youth led to God speaking to his Pastor concerning him becoming the new Youth Pastor. That was in 2009. While serving as Youth Pastor at his church, doors began to open for many speaking a serving engagement for youth all over the State. He felt a "new effective" calling on his life. Then God gave him the unction to start The Flatline Movement. The objective of this ministry is to take the Gospel to the streets of Montgomery and other cities throughout Alabama through the use of music, mentoring/discipleship/, and sports. So, he resigned from his job to answer this call by faith in Jesus.

Then an interesting opportunity recently presented itself when Dewayne was asked if Flatline would sponsor one of Montgomery's top high school AAU basketball teams. He has been able to hold Bible studies with this elite group of high school basketball players.

God saw fit to move him to Strong Tower at Washington Park in Montgomery, AL as their new youth pastor. It made since he became the Chaplain for Carver High School Football team which was the community high school. He is also the Ministry Resident for Montgomery Baptist Association where he serves now.

Made in the USA
Columbia, SC
25 June 2018